ALL THINGS PUPPIES & DOGS FOR KIDS

FILLED WITH FACTS, PHOTOS, AND FUN TO LEARN ALL ABOUT PUPPIES & DOGS

ANIMAL READS

D1464954

WWW.ANIMALREADS.COM

THIS BOOK BELONGS TO...

_____

_____

CONTENTS

WELCOME TO THE WONDERFUL WORLD OF DOGS!

Did you know that, right now, experts think there are almost 900 MILLION dogs and puppies running around our world? What's more, less than half of these are kept as pets in people's homes. The rest are known as 'free-ranging dogs' or, as we know them best, stray dogs.

The most popular pet on earth is also the most beloved. Dogs are incredible animals that have been keeping us company, helping us, and also working for us *for thousands of years*. It's no surprise that we often call them 'man's best friend' but, in reality, they are also woman's best friend, and *definitely* children's best friend too.

If you've picked up this book, it's probably because you love dogs as much as we do. We think these might just be the most adorable, fun, clever, and loving creatures on our planet. Wouldn't you agree?

Yet if you look beyond their playfulness and cuteness, you will discover that the wonderful world of dogs is actually very interesting. Dogs and puppies may be our favorite playmates today, and we may think we know all there is to know about them. Yet dogs remain among the most fascinating and mysterious creatures living on our planet.

WHY ARE DOGS SO SPECIAL?

Over a very (very) long time, dogs have gone from wild creatures to domesticated treasures. They have gone from living in the wilderness to taking over our homes and couches. This is what's known as a *domesticated* animal, one who now lives happily alongside humans.

Dogs live in our homes and sit on our laps; they lick our faces and wag their tails when they are happy. Some get crazy excited when we play with them, and many are very protective of their homes and human families. Scientists have learned that dogs enjoy our company as much as we enjoy theirs.

There's really no other animal on earth that is *all that.*

But there is so much more to dogs than waggy tails and slobbery kisses. Indeed, dogs and puppies may be the most domesticated animal out there, but there is a lot about them that remains quite wild to this day.

Understanding how dogs went from wild canines to couch potatoes will make you appreciate dogs and puppies even more, we promise!

Ready to jump right into the amazing world of dogs and learn all there is to know about these incredible creatures?

LET'S GO!

DOGS ARE MY
FAVORITE PEOPLE!

WHAT ARE DOGS?

Dogs are animals of the species *Canis lupus familiaris*, and they belong to a family of animals called canids. This family also includes wolves, jackals, coyotes, and foxes.

In fact, the modern 'dog' originates from the wild grey wolves that roamed Europe or Asia many moons ago. Experts don't even know exactly *where* the first wolves were tamed.

Although they were once **carnivores** (*meaning they mostly only ate meat*), dogs have now become **omnivores** (*meaning they eat just about anything!*)

This change in their diet has happened over thousands of years, as wild dogs became used to living with us humans and, eventually, eating everything we ate.

Experts believe dogs were domesticated around 15,000–20,000 years ago. That is one heck of a long time, right? Since early humans started domesticating early dogs, the two species have formed a very special bond. We have other domesticated pets in our lives today, like cats for example, but none share the kind of deep bond we have with dogs.

It is important to remember, however, that we must always respect dogs and their personal space. Even the cutest, furriest doggo is not always looking for a hug or a pat, so we have to keep this in mind, right?

Dogs may be man's best friend, but they are animals, after all, with instincts we still can't fully predict, and strength we cannot even begin to imagine.

Despite the fact we have domesticated dogs for a long time, not every member of this family of animals is up for a hug and a kiss. In fact, you should never approach a dog you don't know without asking for the owner's permission. It's always a good idea to have an adult present whenever you interact with a dog.

Yep, even a cute little chihuahua! They may be *smol*, but they can be feisty!

HOW MANY TYPES OF DOGS ARE THERE?

Today, there are about 400 different breeds of dogs on our planet.

How many can you name?

We bet you know quite a few breeds!

You're probably wondering how on earth we ended up with so many different types of dogs in the world, right?

Well, you might be surprised to learn that the majority of these breeds have only been around for about 200 years. Beforehand, there were just *dogs*, but then people noticed that some dogs were very good at certain tasks, like herding a flock of sheep or protecting chickens, so that wild foxes didn't attack them. Others noticed that some dogs were particularly keen to sit on people's laps and just couldn't get enough of human cuddles.

People started breeding similar dogs with very specific *traits* (that's what we call a dog's special talents) in order to create a puppy who would definitely have that trait. This is how we made herding dogs and lapdogs, also terriers, sporting dogs, and even hound dogs.

Over the last 50 years, we have created many different breeds for many different purposes. Some dog breeds are perfect for people who have allergies (because they don't lose a lot of hair), while others are particularly good with children, so they make fantastic family pets.

This is how we eventually ended up with 400 different breeds of dogs!

WHICH DOG ALWAYS KNOWS WHAT TIME IT IS?

A watch dog!

WHAT ARE THE MOST POPULAR DOG DOG BREEDS TODAY?

E ven though there are 400 different breeds of dogs all over the world, 10 remain absolute favorites with people all over the world. Want to know what they are?

Here we go!

LABRADOR RETRIEVER

The Labrador Retriever is the most popular dog breed in American homes, and it's not hard to see why. Labs absolutely *love* people and are often also affectionate to cats, birds, and other pets. Labs have a natural instinct to please people, and that's what makes them ideal pets.

They have webbed feet and are excellent swimmers, which is why they were bred to help fishermen bring in nets and pull ropes in the water. The Labrador has a double coat that is water-resistant, which means they can float much better than other breeds. This is the world's best water dog!

GOLDEN RETRIEVER

Golden Retrievers are also a global favorite and are often mistaken for their Labrador cousins. How can you tell them apart? By the shape of their snout! Goldens have narrower muzzles and don't tend to get the deep jowl that Labradors do. Much like labs, however, they also make awesome family pets. The first ever litter of Golden Retriever puppies was born in 1868, and they were specifically bred to 'retrieve' hunted game.

GERMAN SHEPHERD

The global protectors of *everything and everyone*, German shepherds are used as police dogs the world over. They are active, muscular, highly intelligent, and can be fierce if they need to be. The German shepherd was first bred in...*drum roll please*...Germany! Yet, given this breed can live comfortably in many different places, it has been exported all over the world. This is one of the best search and rescue dogs there is!

BULLDOG

Did you know that bulldogs were originally bred to fight bulls? Now you do! Yep, that's exactly where the name of the breed comes from. Luckily, this pupper's bull-fighting days are long behind him and, today, he can look forward to a comfy life as a favorite family pet. The bulldog has not lost any of its courage through the years, and this, combined with its incredible love and devotion to its family, makes it an amazing guard dog.

BEAGLE

The Beagle is a very sweet dog, with good manners and health that makes it easy to look after. Originally, they were also bred for hunting on the ground, and this is an example of a *hound dog*. They have short legs (so they can sniff the ground), long floppy ears (which help direct smells from the ground towards their nose!), and a white tail that they stick up when they get excited. This acts like a 'white flag' in fields with long grass, so the hunter could see where they were! Beagles are very intelligent, have an amazing sense of smell, and are very focused. That's why many of them have jobs as sniffer dogs in airports or with the police!

FRENCH BULLDOG

Oh, how cute is the French Bulldog?! We know, adorable! Now, the history of this breed is super interesting. Experts believe this breed was first created in England, where it was bred to be a lap dog for women who made lace (this is a beautiful fabric pattern). Their dogs would sit on their laps and keep the women warm. This was a time when lace was mainly made in England. When the lace making moved to France, lace workers brought their lap dogs along, eventually breeding them with local French dogs. And that's how the French Bulldog was born! This is one of the dog breeds made to be companions, first and foremost, so they make perfect family pets. Their job is to cuddle!

ROTTWEILER

Rotties sometimes have a bad reputation for being aggressive. Still, in reality, this is a powerful large dog that was bred to do hard work. This is one of the oldest dog breeds in the world, and it is believed that the ancient Romans used them to herd cattle as they moved across Europe. In Germany, they were used to pull carts full of meat for butchers, and that's why they are known as 'Butcherdogs' (or Metzgerhund in German)! Strong working dogs like the Rottweiler need good training as puppies and, when they receive it, they make amazing companions. They are fiercely loyal and affectionate, and can be very playful too.

SIBERIAN HUSKY

You probably already know that Siberian Huskies are made for cold climates, right? Of course, they are, look at all that fur! This dog breed came from Siberia (a remote region of Russia) and a place that gets *crazy cold* in winter.

For this reason, the husky has a built-in winter coat (wouldn't that be handy?), and because it has been used to pull sleds in snow for such a long time, they have an innate drive to run. This means the desire to run is an instinct they sometimes cannot control.

As a pet, huskies can make great companions, but they need training when young and must be exercised, every day. A husky is born to run, and run it must!

BOXER

Boxers can sometimes look grumpy, but in reality, they are the most playful dog breed there is. In fact, they are known as 'forever puppies' because they just don't seem to ever grow up and end up acting like puppies their entire life.

Yes, this means they *can* be a bit of a handful! The Boxer is a high-energy dog that needs daily exercise and, unlike many other breeds, they become fiercely loyal to a group of people (like a whole family!) and don't only choose one human as its leader.

Boxers are naturally friendly to everyone and are great with both kids and the elderly. Originally bred to fight, the Boxer is still protective today, except now it makes a fantastic guard dog.

DACHSHUND (AKA THE SAUSAGE DOG!)

After learning about the Beagle, you can probably already guess what this long dog with short legs and floppy ears was bred for, right? Yes, this is also a hound dog! Except with the Dachshund, its job was to hunt badgers and other creatures hiding in underground holes. Super playful, the sausage dog can be stubborn and has a habit of chasing small animals. We guess their ancestor traits remain!

WHAT KIND OF DOG IS THE QUIETEST SLEEPER OF ALL?

A hush puppy!

AMAZING FACTS ABOUT DOGS!

Now that you know a little more about dog breeds and their history, it's time to delve into the world of dogs even more. These are truly incredible creatures!

THEIR SENSE OF SMELL IS OFF.THE.CHARTS.

Some dog-owners joke that their pooch can smell food a mile away. In fact, it probably can! Some dogs' sense of smell is around 100,000 times stronger than ours, although it really depends on the breed. The hound-type dogs have the strongest smelling skills, and that's why they are used by airports and the police in many countries!

A DOG'S WET NOSE HELPS IT SMELL BETTER

Have you ever wondered why dogs' noses are always wet? Well, their noses produce a gel-like substance that traps smells, so the dog has more time to figure out what it is! The nose is the first thing a vet will check if a dog seems to be a little bit sick. Sometimes, sickness in dogs comes with a dry and warm nose, so it's always good to check if it's wet and cold to the touch!

DOGS CAN TASTE WHAT THEY SMELL. WAIT...*WHAAAAT*?

Dogs have a special organ on the inside of their mouths that lets them actually taste whatever they smell. This is why they drool when they smell food...they are literally already tasting it in their mouth!

THE SMALL AND TALL OF IT

The tallest dog breed in the world is the Great Dane (and they are indeed GREAT!), while the smallest is the tiny sweet Chihuahua, which usually weighs about 4 pounds!

THE FASTEST GOOD BOY!

The fastest breed is the Greyhound, a tall, long and skinny breed that is built for speed. This fast good boy can run up to 45 miles an hour!

DOGS CAN HAVE ALL SORTS OF JOBS

Nowadays, dogs are used for all manner of jobs. There are therapy dogs (used to make people feel better when they're a bit down) and what's known as service dogs. They help their owners in a variety of ways, from guiding the blind (guide dogs!) to helping detect if a person is about to faint because they have a medical condition (seizure dogs!)

THEIR NOSE PRINTS ARE LIKE OUR HUMAN FINGERPRINTS... UNIQUE!

Now this will throw you for a loop! Did you know that a dog's nose print is unique to that individual, and unlike any other doggo nose print? Now you do! This is just like our human fingerprints!

A DOG'S EAR HAS 18 MUSCLES

Ever notice how a dog can turn its ears in almost every direction? A dog will use its many ear bones to direct its ears towards a specific sound. This helps it figure out two things: one, where the sound is coming from and, two, what it is!

DOGS SWEAT MOSTLY FROM THEIR FEET

Alright, this one is totally loopy, **but true.** Dogs have most of their sweat glands at the bottom of their feet so, although they do sweat a little by panting, most of their sweat pours right out of their paw pads!

PUPPIES NEED LOTS OF LOVE AND CARE

Newborn puppies are born with sealed eyes, so they really don't know what's going on. The eyelids eventually open after two weeks. Pups begin walking upright at 3-5 weeks, and their first teeth come out at 6 weeks. This is also the stage at which a puppy's ears open, and they can finally hear all the cooing sounds you're making! Amazingly, puppies can sleep up to 19 hours a day, so it's really important to let them have their rest.

WE ARE STILL LEARNING MORE ABOUT DOGS

They may be our companions for many years, but there is still a lot we are learning about dogs. In recent years, it has been discovered that some dogs can smell disease and that they see in a few different colors, even though we thought they saw the world in black and white. What's more, researchers discovered that dogs really are *very smart*, even as smart as a 2 or 3-year-old child.

"DOGS LEAVE PAWPRINTS ON OUR HEARTS"

WHAT MAKES DOGS UNIQUE

WHAT FEATURES DO DOGS HAVE?

Sometimes, it's true: dogs really can look like their owners!

Dogs share many of humans' body characteristics like having a heart to transport blood to the organs, lungs to breathe in oxygen, and a stomach for digesting those yummy treats. But they also have distinct features that set them apart from us.

BODY SIZE

A dog's body comes in different shapes and sizes.

The smallest dogs, especially the toy and miniature kinds, weigh between five and 10 pounds, medium-sized ones? They weigh between 10 and 50 pounds. Dogs on the larger side, like retrievers and shepherds, weigh between 65 and 100 pounds.

The biggest ones, or the XXL ones like Mastiff or St. Bernard, can weigh as much as 200 pounds. That's almost as heavy as two adult people combined!

METABOLISM

A dog's metabolism is higher than ours. Do you know what a "metabolism" is? It's how quickly your body turns your food into energy! That's why dogs have more energy than most of us. Because of this though, they age faster, too.

Dogs don't live as long as people. For the first two years of a dog's life, one dog year is equal to 10 to 12 human years. Then after this, it turns into 4 human years per dog year. So, really, a dog turns into a 'teenager' when it's about 18 months old!

TEMPERATURE

Dogs can retain the heat in their bodies much better than we can. Even breeds that were not bred in cold climates can manage cold temperatures really well. The problem, in fact, comes when it gets very hot.

Because dogs don't sweat like we do, they can run into problems when it gets too hot. If a dog is panting a lot, it is taking shorter breaths which can make it hard for its heart to work properly. Dogs should always have access to cold drinking water and a shady place to rest.

SIGHT

Dogs can see better than humans do, especially at nighttime. Their eyes have reflective layers that magnify light. This enables them to see more accurately, even when it's dark. Also, dogs have a third eyelid, which protects their eyes from scratches. This is how dogs can travel through bushes without hurting their eyes!

HEARING

Dogs also hear much better than people. These magical 4-legged friends actually hear 4 times better than us on average! They can listen to sounds with higher frequencies than most of us cannot detect. They can also quickly tell where most sounds are coming from. Because of all those clever bones!

Dogs developed these useful hearing traits over the years to become good at hunting. But, having sensitive hearing makes their ears prone to infection. That's why it's important to clean the ears of many dog breeds to prevent wax or buildup!

SMELL

By now, you know that dogs have a fantastic sense of smell. One whiff of beef jerky is enough to make them scurry into the kitchen in mere seconds! This sharp sense of smell is also why dogs are great at following criminals' tracks to help with police work. They're perfect assistants for the job!

TASTE

Dogs tend to open their mouths when they are smelling something, and this helps them determine if it will be good to eat or not. Despite this clever trait, their taste buds are not as sharp as people's. Dogs may not be able to enjoy a piece of steak by experiencing all the flavors as we do. Still, they sure think it's just as heavenly when they catch its scent from afar!

PAWS AND NAILS

A dog's paws have pads underneath to protect them when they touch the ground. They provide the paws grip on slippery surfaces and help them run long miles without getting blistered.

Their nails are made for digging and give them traction while running. That's why part of dog grooming includes nail trimming to make sure they don't easily break or curl around.

SKIN AND FUR

A dog's skin is much more sensitive than human skin — that's why you can't just use any shampoo to bathe them. Special shampoos protect their skin! A dog's fur draws oils from its skin, which makes it shiny and sort of waterproof. Most dogs shed their hair throughout the year, especially during the spring and fall. A dog's fur is made to protect them against the cold as it provides additional insulation.

In fact, this is so crucial to many working dogs that some are never washed at all!

TEETH AND TONGUE

Dogs' teeth are made for tearing meat, much like their wolf ancestors. A puppy has 28 baby teeth, while a full-grown dog has 43 adult ones. Their teeth have different jobs. The front teeth are meant to grab and tear food, while the ones at the back are made to grind it into smaller bits before swallowing.

A dog's mouth has saliva, or spit, to soften food. The tongue helps bring food to the back of the throat, lick up small pieces, and lap up water.

WHAT'S A **DOG'S** FA**VOR**ITE KIND OF PIZZA?

Pupperoni!

WHAT DO DOGS EAT?

Dogs commonly eat dog food called kibble — those brown-colored, pellet-shaped things. Those are made of ground-up foods like meat, grains, veggies, and fruits.

Because various breeds have evolved to be unique, not every dog can eat the same things. Some dogs eat human food alongside their kibble, while others don't tolerate it as much.

Like people, it also comes down to the individual. Generally speaking, most dogs will eat everything they get their chompers on, although not everything is good for them.

Here are some human foods that we **CAN** safely share with dogs:

- Bread
- Rice
- Corn
- Cheese
- Eggs
- Popcorn
- Yogurt
- Milk
- Peanut butter

Here are some human foods we should **NOT** share with dogs. These can make dogs very sick:

- Chocolate
- Cinnamon
- Ice cream
- Lemons
- Onions
- Garlic
- Salty foods
- Almonds
- Macadamia nuts

I WILL ALWAYS WOOF YOU!

THE LIFE CYCLE OF DOGS

Puppies grow into teenagers and then later into full-grown adults. As dogs get older, they can't see very well or hear very well, so they tend to slow down a lot, not play or chase other animals as much.

Pure-bred dogs live up to 11 years, while mixed breeds live up to 13 years. The average lifespan of dogs depends on the breed, how healthy their families are, and how much love and care they have been given over the course of their lives.

PUPPY STAGE: 0 TO 18 MONTHS

The puppy stage starts from the day puppies are born until they turn 6 to 18 months old.

Puppies should spend a lot of time with their moms and siblings until they are 8 weeks old. This keeps them safe, warm, and regularly fed.

After 8 weeks, if the puppies are going into a human home, they will receive their shots from the vet to make sure they grow up healthy.

TEENAGER STAGE: 18 TO 36 MONTHS

The teenager stage starts somewhere between 6 to 18 months and lasts until 24 months for small dogs or 36 months for large ones. This is the stage where a dog experiences bodily changes that can make them moody — just like human teenagers!

Teenage dogs may not pay as much attention to commands and can even act out, showing challenging behavior. They may also become more active and start exploring everything around them more often than usual.

A dog's teenage stage is the perfect time to help them develop good behavior, and that's why good training is important at this stage.

ADULT STAGE: 2 TO 3 YEARS ONWARD

The adult stage starts at 2 years for small dogs and 3 years for big ones. This is when dogs become easier to be around, showing good behavior they developed during training.

Adult dogs enjoy walks, daily play, and activities that help make them smarter. Remember that dogs need exercise. If you have a dog, don't forget to take them out for a walk, hike or play in the park, so they stay strong and healthy.

SENIOR STAGE: 7 TO 10 YEARS ONWARD

The senior stage starts from 7 to 10 years old. You know a dog has reached the senior stage when its muzzle starts to turn gray. They will also prefer slow and quiet walks rather than the usual energetic play. They tend to sleep a lot, too. This is also when they need to go to the vet more often to get their checkups.

We know we've said that dogs live only up to 11 to 13 years, but some dogs make it past 20 years! This depends partly on nature and partly on how well we take care of them, like the foods we give and the amount of exercise they get.

A 3 month old and a 12 year old golden retriever.

HOLD IT RIGHT THERE PAW'TNER!

HAVING A DOG AS A PET

If you are such a dog lover, you have probably already hounded your family about getting a dog, right? We know, we know, they would make a wonderful friend!

Yet owning a dog is a lot of work and responsibility. Plus, you really should get a dog whose *traits* fit with your life. We can't simply choose a dog because of its looks!

So, to help you and your family make the right decision, let's take a closer look...

DO I WANT A SMALL DOG OR A BIG DOG?

While small dogs are great for kids, that doesn't mean big dogs aren't, too. They are both perfect, depending on what you can handle.

The good thing about small dogs is you can easily carry them around and take care of them. But, because they are so tiny, they can get injured if you accidentally step on them! Also, they get cold easily, so you have to make an effort to keep them warm.

Big dogs are great companions and are very protective. They like to play around, that's why they need a lot of space to wag their tails! Sometimes, they don't know how big they are, so you have to be careful not to let them walk all over you.

CAN I KEEP UP WITH THEIR ENERGY?

Choosing a dog that's right for you also depends on how much and how often you're willing to play with your furry friend. Some dogs love to stay active, so be prepared to keep up with their high energy. Then, some pups are perfectly happy just staying indoors, watching TV with the entire family.

There's a dog breed to suit every family. The trick is to know which one would live well with yours!

Some dog breeds are more active than others. It really all depends on the dog's personality. Whatever the case may be, you have to make sure you're ready to play with your dog, take them out for walks, and go on adventures with them regularly, so they stay happy and healthy. This applies even to the calmest dog breeds.

HOW DO I TAKE CARE OF IT?

Playing with dogs is one thing, but taking care of them is another story. This includes brushing their hair, bathing them, cleaning up after them, and making sure they're healthy. After all, they're a part of the family! So, they deserve the same love and attention that any member would normally receive.

Every dog's human should be responsible for keeping it clean, safe, and well taken care of. It's not always the adults who should be in charge of maintaining the family dog. Kids should also take part in it. It's a great way to show your love for your dog.

SHOULD I GET A PUPPY OR A FULL-GROWN DOG?

Puppies are always a good choice for kids because they are small, sweet, and super adorable.

Yet puppies need to be trained, so you have to spend a lot of time teaching them how to behave. Without house training, they might end up always getting into trouble, chewing on shoes, peeing on the floor, and breaking furniture. It's ok because you know this phase will pass, but it's still a lot of work, and time is needed for them in the early stages.

On the other hand, full-grown dogs have already developed their energy level and attitude. So, they're an excellent choice if you don't want to spend a lot of time training them. It's all about getting to know them and letting them adjust to their new home.

IS IT BETTER TO GET A PURE BREED OR A MIXED BREED?

Pure-breeds are extremely popular, but that doesn't mean mutts don't deserve our attention. You may be drawn to a specific breed because of how they look or how they're known for a particular personality, and we totally get that.

Yet you should also consider that of all the dogs and puppies in the world, less than half are pets. That means millions of strays are out there, looking for a good home. Your nearest pet shelter probably has many dogs who are desperately looking for a home!

Have you heard of the slogan *adopt don't shop*'? This is a wonderful initiative that was created to highlight the struggle of homeless pets, dogs in particular.

Perhaps, given you love dogs so much, you might want to talk about adopting a dog from your nearest shelter with your whole family.

Whatever the case may be, we are confident that you're going to give your pupper the best life he or she deserves. Don't forget to flip back to the pages to remind yourself of the things you've come across. Or better yet, you can read this book again (and again) to serve as your ultimate guide for understanding and taking the best care of your dog.

We wish you many happy memories with your furry friend! We are sure you're going to enjoy walking in the park together, playing fetch, exploring the rest of the world, and simply being there for each other!

WHAT DO YOU CALL A MAGICAL DOG?

A labra-cadabra-dor!

HOW TO TRAIN YOUR DOG

When you get a new dog, it's kind of like adopting a baby — the little one has a lot to learn. You have to teach it how to do things like to sit or stay. Training your dog can be challenging, but it can also feel great once you see them behaving well. Here are some tips on how to train your dog:

STAY CONSISTENT

With dog training, consistency is key. This means letting your dog know when they're not supposed to do something and praising them whenever they're doing something right — every time.

One common mistake of humans is not following through on rewarding their dogs for good behavior. Without letting them know they're a "good boy or girl" or giving them a treat each time, how will dogs understand they're doing what they're supposed to?

So don't be shy and shower your 4 legged friend with plenty of praise! When they are behaving well, of course.

BE INVOLVED

Training dogs is more effective when it involves the whole family. Adults and kids alike can take part in encouraging their dogs to behave well — and stop chewing on the furniture!

Getting everyone involved in training the dog brings families closer together. Dogs can feel that, too. When they're in a nurturing environment, they'll grow up happier and healthier.

TURN YOUR BACK

Yes, that's right. Turn your back on your dog — when they keep jumping, that is. If your dog keeps doing this whenever they see you or new people, this means they want attention.

The trick is to turn your back and allow your dog to sit first. Once that happens, give your pet a treat. If not, keep your back turned and wait until your dog settles down.

Repeat this process when necessary, and your dog will catch on quickly.

USE WORD COMMANDS

When training your dog to learn new things, it is important to use word commands. Words like "sit," "come," and "stay" are common words to use.

Use word commands with a firm tone and hand gestures, so your dog will know exactly what you want every time. Saying "good boy" or "good girl" lets your dog know you're pleased with what they're doing.

Also, dogs can sense emotions. They'll know when you're not happy with what they did. Just remember to go easy on them, because just like humans, they can feel hurt, too.

GIVE TREATS & STAY POSITIVE

You don't want your dog to like the treats in your hand more than you. One important dog-training secret is to teach pups to want to be with you as much as they want the goodies you have in your hand.

To do this, wait for your dog to sit when he or she sees you. This way, you're teaching your pet to do something first before receiving the treat. In this case, it's sitting or behaving properly.

Doing this trick will help you give your pup a double treat: hanging out with you and the goodie you have in your hand.

MY BEST FRIEND HAS FUR AND A TAIL!

DOGS WILL ALWAYS BE MAN'S BEST FRIEND

Dogs are extraordinary creatures. We consider them "earth's little angels" because they spread love and happiness wherever they go. They are very loyal and always love you for who you are. They are not just pets but family members. That's why they deserve all the love and care in the world.

Dogs are born to help people. They are excellent guides for those who can't see or hear and warm, fluffy companions for those who are often sad. Some do police work really well, while others make great search-and-rescue team members. Dogs are heroes because they help make people's lives better every day.

You may already have a pup to take care of or are still thinking of adopting one. Whatever the case is, we hope this book has helped you learn more about dogs and how to take care of them. Just reading this book is a clear sign that you're going to be a great family member and friend to your dog!

We are confident that you're going to give your pupper the best life he or she deserves. Don't forget to flip back to the pages to remind yourself of the things you've come across. Or better yet, you can read this book again (and again) to serve as your ultimate guide for taking the best care of your dog.

We wish you many happy memories with your furry friend! We are sure you're going to enjoy walking in the park together, playing fetch, exploring the rest of the world, and simply being there for each other!

DON'T STOP

RETRIEVIN'!

THANK YOU!

Thank you for reading this book and for allowing us to share our love for dogs with you!

If you've enjoyed this book, please let us know by leaving a rating and a brief review wherever you made your purchase! This helps us spread the word to other readers!

Thank you for your time, and have an *paw*esome day!

For more information, please visit:

www.animalreads.com

HAVE A
HAIRY
DAY!

Published by Admore Publishing: Roßbachstraße, Berlin, Germany

www.admorepublishing.com

REFERENCES

Interested in learning more about dogs?

Check out some of these great resources online. Some of the information on these pages were even used to help create this book.

- https://www.akc.org/expert-advice/lifestyle/dog-facts/
- https://www.britannica.com/animal/dog
- https://www.goodhousekeeping.com/life/pets/g5138/best-family-dogs/
- https://www.homeopet.com/why-mutts-are-awesome
- https://www.thesprucepets.com/how-to-choose-the-right-dog-1117320

- https://www.newscientist.com/article/ 2264329-humans-may-have- domesticated-dogs-by-accident-by- sharing-excess-meat/
- https://www.akc.org/expert-advice/ nutrition/human-foods-dogs-can- and-cant-eat/
- https://www.barkingmad.uk.com/blog/ uncategorised/the-key-stages-of-a-dogs- life-cycle/
- https://www.akc.org/expert-advice/ training/how-to-teach-your-kids-to- train-the-dog/
- https://parenting.firstcry.com/articles/ dog-information-for-kids-50-facts-your- child-must-know/
- https://www.embracepetinsurance.com/ waterbowl/article/dog-training- vocabulary

Printed in Great Britain
by Amazon

82398569R00051